Doctor Jokes

Compiled by a

Doctor

For the

Doctored

By

Amrinder Bajaj

DK's Books For All

Delhi

First Published 2011

ISBN 10: 81-7386-285-0
ISBN 13: 978-81-7386-285-4

Published by
DK's BOOKS FOR ALL
A-6, Nimri Commercial Centre,
Ashok Vihar Phase-IV
Delhi-110052
Phone: 011-27302453, Fax: 011-47061936
e-mail: info@Lppindia.com
website: www.Lppindia.com

Printed at:
D K Fine Art Press P Ltd.
Delhi-110052

PRINTED IN INDIA

Dedicated to

The master raconteur

of our times

Khushwant Singh

A Prayer

From inability to let alone; from too much zeal for the new and contempt for the old, from putting knowledge before wisdom and science before art and cleverness before commonsense; from treating patients as cases; and from making the cure of the disease more grievous than the endurance of the same, God deliver us.

Sir Robert Hutchison

In acknowledgment of the unknown wit that made this work possible.

In gratitude for the gift of humour that makes life livable.

In wonder at the origin of such rollicking hilarity I begin with

A Short History of Medicine

Patient: *"Doctor, I have an ear ache."*

Doctor: *2000 B.C. - "Here, eat this root."*

1000 B.C. - "That root is heathen, say this prayer."

1850 A.D. - "That prayer is superstition, drink this potion."

1940 A.D. - "That potion is snake oil, swallow this pill."

1985 A.D. - "That pill is ineffective, take this antibiotic."

2000 A.D. - "That antibiotic is artificial. Here, eat this root!"

Contents

Part 1 - General

Part 11 – Specialists

PART 1
General

Definitions

A doctor is a person who kills your ills with his pills and you with his bills.

A specialist is one who knows more and more about less and less till he knows almost everything about almost nothing.

Q. What's the difference between a general practitioner and a specialist?

A. One treats what you have; the other thinks you have what he treats.

A pathologist is one who sits on one stool and examines another.

A gynaecologist is one who looks for problems at places where others look for pleasure.

Anaesthetist is a person who is half asleep bending over a person half awake.

An urologist is a person who washes his hands *before* he passes urine.

'If it is dry, moisten it; if it is moist, dry it.' Congratulations, now you are a dermatologist.

Neurotics build castles in the air.
Psychotics live in them.
Psychiatrists collect the rent.

He is not dead; he is electroencephalographically challenged.

The four stages of getting sick: ill, pill, bill and will.

First aid is when you have AIDS for the first time.'

General

Does an apple a day really keep the doctor away?
If you aim it well enough!

An apple a day keeps the doctor away,
But if the doctor is cute keep the apple away.

Doctor: "Do not take alcohol. It is a slow death."
Patient: "I am in no hurry to die."

"The doctor said he would have me on my feet in two weeks."

"And did he?"

"Yes, I had to sell the car to pay his bill."

Nurse: Doctor, the man you've just treated collapsed on the front step what should I do?

Doctor: Turn him around so it looks like he was just arriving.

Prisoner: "Doc! You've already removed my spleen, tonsils, adenoids, and one of my kidneys. I only came to see if you could get me out of this place!"

Doctor: "I am - bit by bit."

Patient: "I feel so sick I wish I could die."

Doctor: "Don't worry. I'll take care of that."

Doctors doing research on the components of beer arrived at a peculiar conclusion. Results revealed that beer contained small amounts of female hormones! To prove this they fed 12 pints of beer to 100 men. All of them started talking nonsense and could not drive!

A man tapped the driver of his taxi on the shoulder to give him directions. At this the taxi driver started, the vehicle skidded, barely missed hitting an oncoming truck and stopped on a sand bank.

"How could a mere tap on the shoulder startle you so?" demanded the customer angrily.

"I am sorry." replied the taxi driver, "I have recently started driving a taxi. For years I used to drive a funeral van."

Doctor: "Do you know that researchers have discovered that diarrhoea is hereditary."

Patient: "Really?"

Doctor: "Yes. It runs in your jeans."

A peculiarly scary thing was happening in a hospital's ICU. Every Sunday with unfailing regularity patients on bed number 5 died at 11 AM every Sunday morning. This puzzled the doctors and some even thought that it had something to do with the supernatural. To investigate the cause of such bizarre incidents, the doctors and nurses decided to keep strict vigilance. A few minutes before 11 AM, the part time Sunday sweeper arrived. Whistling cheerfully, he unplugged the life support system of bed no 5 and put the plug of his vacuum cleaner in its place!

Patient: "Doctor, doctor my wooden leg is giving me a headache."

Doctor: "How is that possible?"

Patient: "My wife keeps hitting me on the head with it."

A fat lady on the phone: "Doctor, please give me something to lose weight. My husband has given me a wonderful present and I cannot get into it.

Doctor: "Come to the clinic tomorrow and I will prescribe something so that you get into the dress."

Patient: "But doctor my husband has bought me a car.

A girl brought home a man who was naked except for a loincloth. He had a painted face, feathered headgear and a spear in one hand.

"Father I have married the type of man you always wanted me to marry."

One look at his son-in-law and the father recoiled in horror.

"I had asked you to marry a 'rich' doctor not a 'witch doctor'!" he sputtered.

A tribal emissary went to a doctor and said:

"Big Chief no shit."

The doctor gave him medicine for the chief's constipation. The emissary returned the next day and exclaimed:

"Big shit no Chief."

One lady to another:

"You must see my doctor."

"But there is nothing wrong with me."

"He is so good that he will find something."

First patient: "If you think that the treatment is expensive you should see my doctor. He is very reasonable."

Second patient: "How's that."

First patient: "If you cannot afford the treatment he alters the reports."

The wife of a wealthy man fell unconscious.

"Quick, give her artificial respiration." the doctor told his resident.

"No way." said her husband. "I don't go for anything artificial. Give her the real thing."

A drunk went to the doctor and said, “I feel tired all the time, my head hurts, and I cannot sleep. What is it, Doc?” The doctor examined him thoroughly and said, “I can’t find anything wrong. It must be the drinking.” “Fair enough,” replied the drunk, “I’ll come back when you’re sober.”

A rabbit escaped from a research laboratory where he had lived since birth. He joined a group of wild rabbits and lived their lives for a day. He fed on juicy carrots, fat lettuces and sighed with pleasure.

“This is life!” He exclaimed.

“So you are going to live with us?” asked the others.

“I wish I could but I really must get back to the laboratory. I am dying for a cigarette.”

During the anti-smoking campaign, a social worker stood by man who was smoking and said: “Do you realize that one third of the cigarette between your lips is being smoked by me.”

“In that case,” replied the man, “You owe me one third of the cost.”

A woman called up the hospital and said, "I want to know if the patient Rita Berry in Room No 1814 is getting better."

The RMO replied, "She is doing very well. She had her first solid meal today, her blood pressure is fine and if she continues improving she might even be sent home in a couple of days."

The woman said, "Thank God! That's wonderful news!"

RMO: "I take it you must be a family member or a close friend!"

"No I am Rita Berry. No one tells me anything!"

Good News and Bad News

An artist asked the gallery owner if anyone had shown interest in her paintings.

"I have good news and bad news for you." he replied. "The good news is that a man asked me if the value of the paintings would appreciate after your death. When I assured him they would, he bought all the 15 paintings."

"That's wonderful but what is the bad news?"

"That man was your doctor!"

A patient woke up following an operation to find the doctor standing at the foot of the bed. "Doctor, how did it go?

"I have good news and bad news", says the doctor.

"Give me the good news, I feel terrible and need cheering up"

"The good news is that we managed to save your testicles"

"That's terrific. What's the bad news?"

"They are under your pillow."

Alarmed by the prolonged discussions of his case by a group of doctors by his bedside, a patient said:

"There must be something terribly wrong with me."

"Why do you say that?" asked the doctor.

"All the other doctors seem to disagree with your diagnosis."

"Don't you worry." consoled the doctor. 'In a similar case sometime back I stood firm on my diagnosis and the postmortem proved me right!"

Doctor to patient"

"Your case will enrich medical sciences."

"O dear! And I thought I'll just have to pay Rs.10000."

"Doctor, I just dropped in to tell you how much I benefited from your treatment."

"As far as I know you are no patient of mine," replied the doctor.

"I know, but my uncle was and I am his heir."

After an annual check up, the doctor told a man that he has a mixed report to give.

"First the good news - your penis has grown 4 inches."

"That's great Doc. What is the bad news?"

"It's malignant!" replied the doctor.

Immediately after his annual examination, a man with a multitude of problems asked anxiously

"Doctor, how do I stand?"

"That's what puzzles me!" replied the doctor.

The doctor took his patient into a room and said, "I have some good news and some bad news."

Patient: "Give me the good news first."

"They're going to name a disease after you."

After examining a patient the doctor took his wife aside and told her that her husband was gravely ill but there were 3 things she could do to ensure his survival.

1. Give him three nutritious meals every day.
2. Do not nag him.
3. Make love to him every night.

While driving back home the husband asked his wife:

"What did the doctor say?"

"I am sorry dear but he said that are not going to make it."

Doctor to patient: "I have good news and bad news for you."

Patient: "Tell me the bad news first."

Doctor: "You will die of cancer within two years."

Patient: "What news could be good after this?"

Doctor: "You have got Dementia's and will soon forget what I told you!"

Doctor: "I have some bad news and some very bad news."

Patient: "Might as well give me the bad news first."

Doctor: "The lab called with your test results. They said you have 24 hours to live."

Patient: "24 HOURS! That's terrible!! WHAT could be WORSE?"

Doctor: "I've been trying to reach you since yesterday."

A man hadn't been feeling well and went for a complete check up. After examining him the doctor told him:

"I'm afraid I have some bad news. You're dying and you don't have much time."

"That's terrible. How long have I got?" asked the man.

"10..." said the doctor.

"10? 10 what, months, weeks? What?!" he enquired frantically.

"10...9...8...7..."

Two retired cricketers were sitting on the porch of an old peoples' home and wondering if they had cricket in heaven. A few days later one of them died and went to heaven. Several days later, the other old man was sitting on the porch when his dead friend appeared by his side and said:

"I have good news and bad news for you. The good news is that they have cricket in heaven."

"That's good. What's the bad news?"

"You are joining the team tonight!"

Mr. Lal went to the Doctor's surgery to collect his wife's test results.

Receptionist: "I'm sorry Sir but there has been a bit of a mix up and we have a problem. When we sent the samples from your wife to the lab, the samples from another Mrs. Lal went as well and we are now uncertain which one is your wife."

Mr. Lal: "So what is the problem?"

Receptionist: "Well the news is either bad or terrible."

Mr. Lal: "What do you mean?"

Receptionist: "Well one Mrs. Lal has tested positive for Alzheimer's and the other for AIDS. We cannot tell which one is your wife."

Mr. Lal: "What am I supposed to do now?

Receptionist: "The doctor recommended that you drop her off in the middle of town and if she finds her way home, don't go to bed with her."

Medical Students

A young man applied for admission to a Medical College but he never made it through the medical entrance test. To guess the reason why, read his answer paper.

DEFINE THE FOLLOWING

1. Antibody - against everybody.
2. Benign - what you will be after eight.
3. Cardiology - advanced study of card playing.
4. Chronic - neck of a crow.
5. Coma - punctuation mark.
6. Cortisone - area around the court.
7. Cyst - short for sister.
8. Diagnosis - person with a slanted nose.
9. Dislocation - in this place.

10. False labour - pretending to work.
11. Hymen - saying 'Hi' to many men.
12. Lymph - walk unsteadily.
13. Microbes - small dressing gown.
14. Protein - in favour of teens.
15. Tumour - an extra pair.
16. Urine - opposite of 'you're out'.
17. Vas deferens -extremely difficult.
18. Caesarean section - a neighborhood in Rome
19. Labor pain - getting hurt at work
20. Seizure - a famous Roman emperor
21. Terminal illness - airport sickness
22. Ultrasound - a loud noise

A teacher was giving a lecture. He said, "In India a woman gives birth to a child every 10 seconds."

Alarmed, a medical student got up and said: "We must find this woman and stop her."

While taking rounds, a doctor examined an X-ray with a group of medical students. "As you can see," she said,

"The patient limps because his left fibula and tibia are radically arched. Reddy, what would you do in a case like this?"

"Well," pondered Reddy, "I suppose I'd limp too."

A student was being interviewed for admission in medical college.

"Tell me,' asked the interviewer," where do you expect to be five years from now?"

"Well let me see," replied the student. "It's Friday. I guess I'll be seeing the first show of the latest movie in town."

Medical student, unable to elicit a response from a patient in coma:

"I have been trying to arouse her for the last half an hour but am unable to do so."

Some examples of history taking by interns:

- "No history of suicide in the past."
- "Patient unable to get pregnant with husband. Has come for a work up."
- "Patient has pain in her abdomen while lying on her left for the past six months."

- "The patient experienced sudden pain in chest while having sex which continued in the emergency room."
- "Patient wringing her hands and biting her nails alternatively. She also appears anxious."
- "Patient had anorexia for lunch."
- "Patient was healthy and well till the bus he was traveling in collided with a tree."
- "The patient slipped and her legs went in different directions last summer."

Professor to his assistant: "Between you and me, we ought to be able to get this lady pregnant."

The professor of anatomy was addressing a new batch of medical students:

"Now that you have joined this profession you must have a strong heart and keen observation and be prepared for anything."

After this he put a finger in a bowl of vomit and licked it. He then asked one student to step forward and repeat the procedure. After much hesitation the student complied.

"Where is your observation young man? Didn't you see that I put in my index finger and licked my middle finger?"

A resident was taking the history of a patient.

'What is your problem?' he asked.

'Shortness of breath.' replied the patient.

'SOB' wrote the resident for short.

The patient saw what was written and exclaimed:

'How dare you call me a son of a bitch!'

A resident was asked the diagnosis of the case during ward rounds. Hurriedly he looked at the chart and said:

"Sir he is a case of F..... hypertension."

"Mind your language young man. Just what do you mean by that?"

"Sir, I suppose he gets high blood pressure immediately after intercourse." stammered the young man.

"Give me the case file." thundered the professor.

The patient was a follow up case (FUC) of Hypertension!

A hopeful medical entrant walked out of an interview in a huff.

When asked why he said indignantly:

"They asked me show my testimonials!"

A physics professor was discussing a particularly complicated concept. A pre-med student rudely interrupted to ask,

"Why do we need such pointless information?'

"To save lives." said the professor and continued his talk.

"So how does physics help save lives?"

"It keeps ignoramuses like you out of medical school."

A frog went to an astrologer to have his future told.

The astrologer said, "Soon you are going to meet a beautiful girl who will want to know all about you."

The frog said, "That's wonderful. Where will I meet her? "

"On the dissection table."

An examiner was taking anatomy practical exams of a boy. With the rest of the body completely draped the examiner held a pointer towards an organ and asked the student what is it? Try as he might the hapless fellow couldn't identify the structure. Wanting to help, the examiner gave a hint:

"It's something neither you nor I have."

Prompt came the reply: "Brains Sir!"

Examiner: "What are the advantages of breast milk?"

Medical student:

- "It is the best form of nutrition available to an infant.
- It is always available at the right temperature.
- It does not get rancid.
- The cat cannot get into it and
- It comes in such nice containers.

A brand new doctor would walk with a swagger, his white medical coat slung over his shoulder, to the local *paan* shop and bask in the respect that all and sundry showered upon him.

One day the paan-wallah asked surprised:

"What is this doctor sahib? You have a white petticoat on your shoulder in place of the coat!"

"Goodness gracious! Both hang on the same peg!"

Nurses

Some reports by nurses:

- By the time he was admitted, his rapid heart beating had stopped, and he was feeling better.
- On the second day the knee was better and on the third day it had completely disappeared.
- She has no rigors or chills now, but her husband said that she was very hot in bed last night.
- I have suggested that he loosen his pants before standing, and then, when he stands with the help of his wife they should fall to the floor.

On her rounds the matron waylaid a junior nurse and asked her.

Where did you give the intra-muscular injection to this child?

"In the admission room."

Matron to nurse: "Wake up that patient; it is time for his sleeping pills."

A nurse walked up to a post operative patient, cleaned a bit of skin with spirit and jabbed in an injection so fiercely that he almost passed out in agony.

"What was that?" he gasped.

"A painkiller." She replied.

A patient in the psychiatrist wards was walking around with her breasts exposed when the matron came in and exploded in anger.

"It's the ward boy," stammered the nurse, "He never puts things back in place after using them."

Doctor to nurse: "Did the patient with the infected wound come to the OPD today."

Nurse "Yes. As she was fine today so I sent her home without dressing."

Doctor: "Why did you let them take away the body?"

Nurse: "Because patient refused an autopsy."

Doctor: Have you X Rayed the patient?
X Ray technician: "Yes Sir, the patient was X rated."

Doctor: "Why did you send me an emergency call?"
Nurse: "Because the patient feels numb from toes downwards."

Call sent by nurse to the resident doctor: "Patient unable to pass urine, please come and pass."

A doctor's secretary was having trouble with the doctor's notes on an emergency case, which read, 'Shot in the lumbar region'. The poor girl was at her wits' end. After much thought she figured it out and typed, "Wounded in the woods."

The nurse went in to check a patient in the ICU, who has nasal prongs inserted in his nostrils. The nurse tried to talk to him, but all she could get out of him was gasping and unintelligible talk. Finally, the nurse thrust a note pad and pencil at the patient and said, "I can't understand you, sir. Please write it down."
The patient weakly scribbled on the pad, "Get your foot off my oxygen tube!"

Patient to X-ray technician after swallowing some money:
"Do you see any change in me?"

On seeing a patient with chills and rigors the alarmed nurse sent a call to the doctor stating:
"Come soon. Patient is doing something, something under the blanket."

A doctor questioned a student nurse:
"How will you know that the water for a baby's bath is of the right temperature?"
"If the baby turns blue it is cold, if he turns red it is hot and if he retains his original colour the temperature is right." She rattled off in one breath.

A doctor was treating a man who had imbibed too much alcohol. Before retiring for the night he instructed the nurse:
"Give him the same medicine if he sees green snakes again."
When the doctor returned in the morning the patient was raving. Enraged he asked the nurse:
"Why didn't you repeat the medicines?"
Nurse" "But he didn't see green snakes, he saw pink elephants."

Pharmacist

Customer: Have you anything for gray hair?"

Chemist: "Nothing but the greatest respect."

A boy was trying in vain to get his girl friend to sleep with him. She finally promised to do so if he came to meet her family. Eagerly anticipating the union, he rushed to a pharmacist and bought a packet of condoms. After grace, the rest of the family began eating but the boy refused to raise his head.

"I did not know you were so devout." whispered the girl admiringly.

"And I did not know that your father was a pharmacist." hissed the boy.

A lady waited patiently at the pharmacist till he was free to serve her. At last he asked:

"May I help you madam?"

"Could you please read this letter from my fiancé for me? He is a doctor!"

A man went to a pharmacist and asked if he had anything for hiccups. Without warning the pharmacist reached over and gave him a smart smack on the back.

"Did that help?" he asked.

"I don't know," replied the startled man. "I'll have to ask my wife. She is the one who has hiccups."

A scientist went to a drug store and asks the pharmacist, "Do you have any acetylsalicylic acid?"

"You mean aspirin?" asked the pharmacist.

"That's it. I can never remember that word."

Upon arriving home a husband was confronted by an outraged wife.

"What is it darling?" he asked alarmed.

"It is the pharmacist; he insulted me on the phone this morning."

Enraged, the husband rang up the drugstore and demanded an explanation.

"Please listen to my side of the story Sir." begged the pharmacist "When I got out of the house this morning I could not find my car keys and realized that I had locked it in the car last night. When I finally managed to trace the duplicate I was already late. Driving too fast I got a speeding ticket. As if this was not enough I had a flat that delayed me still further. My store was full of customers and my assistant hadn't turned up. As I was attending to them, some cash fell out of my drawer. I bent to pick up the change when the phone rang. I got up suddenly to attend it and banged my head against the cash drawer. With my head reeling I picked up the receiver and it was your wife asking me how to use a rectal thermometer. After all this surely you can excuse my saying 'up your....'"

An old man went to the pharmacist with a prescription for Viagra. Painstakingly, he broke a tablet into 4 equal parts and swallowed a quarter with a slug of water.

"What are you doing?" asked the pharmacist intrigued, "You have to take one whole tablet and that too before sex."

"I know but I just want enough so that I do not wet my shoes when I pass urine!" replied the old man.

A man shoved a prescription again towards the pharmacist and asked:

“Are you sure that this medicine has to be taken life long?”

“Yes.”

There was a moment of silence after which the man heaved a huge sigh and said: “I wonder how serious my condition is. It is mentioned on the bottle ‘NO REFILLS’.”

Fitness

Regular naps prevent old age, especially if you take them while driving.

A young woman having a physical examination, felt very embarrassed because of a weight problem. As she removed her last bit of clothing, she said,

"Doctor, I feel so ashamed. I guess I've really let myself go."

"Now, now," the doctor said, as he began to examine her. "Don't feel that way. You really don't look that bad."

"Do you really think so?" she asked.

"Of course," replied the doctor, as he held a tongue depressor in front of her face. "Now, open your mouth wide and say moo!"

One lady friend to another: "You look different today"

"The doctor asked me to lose 5kgs."

"And you lost 5kgs?"

"Yes, I stopped wearing makeup."

A man walked into a doctor's office. He had a cucumber up his nose, a carrot in his left ear and a banana in his right ear.

"What's the matter with me?" he asked the doctor.

The doctor replied, "You're not eating properly."

An irate customer came back to the shop from where he had bought butter half an hour ago.

"Where is my free gift?" he demanded.

"There *is* no free gift with this pack." said the shopkeeper.

"But it reads 'Cholesterol free'."

A doctor put an overweight woman on a diet.

"Eat regular meals for 2 days and then skip a day. I want you to repeat this procedure for two weeks. Next time I see you, you'll have lost at least 5lbs."

When she returned after a fortnight, the doctor was amazed to see that she had lost 20 lbs.!

"Did you follow my instruction?"

"Yes and I nearly died on the third day."

"Of hunger?"

"No, from skipping."

An extremely obese man showed up at his doctor's office and claimed that he had tried every possible way to lose weight, to no avail. So the doctor proposed a radical diet - rectal feeding. Reassuring the fattie that he wouldn't starve to death, the doctor explained that he could actually take in enough nutrients through the rectal walls to sustain life and was sure to lose weight in the process.

Three weeks later the patient came in for a follow-up appointment, and was down from 360 pounds to a trim 175 pounds. The doctor asked him how he was feeling, for he noticed that the fellow was bouncing up and down in his seat quite energetically.

"I'm feeling great, doc; never felt better!"

"In that case, why are you bouncing up and down like that?" asked the doctor.

"Just chewing some gum!"

A man stood on the weighing scales and desperately tired to pull his stomach in.

"That is not going to reduce your weight" observed his wife cuttingly.

"I know. I am only trying to read the scales."

A woman put a coin on the commercial weighing scales measured her weight. Taking off her jacket she put in another coin and was happy to note that she weighed a little less. Thus encouraged, she began shedding her clothes and putting in coins till she ran out of coins. A man, watching the proceedings, walked up to her and said:

"Don't worry about the coins, just keep stripping."

A hugely pregnant woman weighed herself at the weighing machine at railway stations that gives a cute little message along with the weight on a ticket. Hers read:

"One at a time."

On examining a patient the doctor found that all his problems were due to lack of exercise.

"You should run at least ten kilometers per day."

"Just someone I know professionally."

"Your profession or hers?"

Gynecology professor: "What size should the penis be for successful penetration?""

Female student: "Nine inches."

Prof: "I am talking of necessity not luxury."

A gynecologist and a cardiologist had twin daughters. Guess what they named them?

Angina and vagina!

A doctor and his wife were having a big argument at breakfast.

"You aren't so good in bed either!" he shouted and stormed off to work.

By midmorning, he decided he'd better make amends and phoned home. After many rings, his wife picked up the phone.

"What took you so long to answer?"

"I was in bed."

"What were you doing in bed this late?"

"Getting a second opinion."

Doctor 1 "I had sex with my patient. I am feeling guilty."

Doctor 2 "It happens in our profession. Take it easy."

Doctor 1 "But I am a vet!"

At a medical convention, a male and female doctor started eyeing each other. The male doctor asked her to dinner and she accepted. As they sat down at the restaurant, she excused herself to wash her hands.

After dinner, one thing led to another and they ended up in her hotel bedroom. Just as things got hot, the female doctor got up to wash her hands. After the sex session, she washed her hands again.

The male doctor said, "I bet you are a surgeon".

"Yes. How did you know?"

"Easy, you're always washing your hands."

"Right and I bet you're an anesthesiologist."

"Wow, how did you guess?"

"I didn't feel a thing."

Man: "Doc you must help me. Each day I make love twice with my wife, twice with my secretary and twice with my girl friend."

Doc: "So what's your problem?"

Man: "It hurts when I masturbate."

"Doctor how many times in a week can I have sex."

"It depends upon the age but remember the word tri-weekly."

"What do you mean?"

"Well, in the initial stages you can have it tri-weekly. After 40 years of age you can try weekly and, after 50 years try weakly.

A woman brought her husband to the psychiatrist complaining that he wanted to have sex in her ear.

The doctor tried to frighten him by saying that she might become deaf after such an act.

"Well she hasn't become dumb as yet." retorted the husband.

A boy went to see the urologist, complaining of discharge dripping from his penis.

The doctor took one look and told him he had V.D.

"No way, Doc," replied the boy, blushing furiously. "It must be a cold."

"Call it whatever you like," the doctor said, "But until it sneezes, we'll have to treat it for V.D."

A 90 years old man went to his doctor for his yearly physical. A couple of days later, the doctor saw the man walking down the street with a gorgeous young lady on his arm.

When the man returned to the doctor for his follow up visit, the doctor remarked, "You're really doing great, aren't you?"

"I'm doing just what you told me, doctor: 'Get a hot mamma and be cheerful'," the man replied.

"But that's not what I told you," replied the doctor. "I said you have a heart murmur. Be careful!"

A guy walked into the doctor's office for an appointment.

"Would you like to tell me your problem?" asked the pretty receptionist "I'll need to jot down the information."

"It's rather embarrassing," the guy stammered. "You see I have a very large and almost constant erection."

"Well, the doctor is very busy today," the receptionist cooed, "But maybe I could squeeze you in."

A man suffering from laryngitis rang the doctor's doorbell at an odd hour.

"Is the doctor in?" he asked in a hoarse whisper.

"No." said the doctor's wife, "You can come in."

A middle-aged man, Mr. Sharma, underwent a heart surgery. His wife would not allow him to have sex lest it threaten his life. Frustrated, the man went back to his doctor and told him his problem.

"Sex won't kill you." assured the doctor.

"My wife won't believe me. Could you give it in writing?"

The good doctor obliged.

'Dear Mrs. Sharma,' he wrote, 'Your husband is in remarkable physical condition and quite capable of making love twice or thrice a night."

Mr. Sharma was jubilant but requested a slight amendment. "Could you delete Mrs. Sharma and write 'To whom it may concern'?"

"Doctor I think my son had VD." Mr. Gupta told his urologist on phone. "The only one he did it with is the maid."

Dr. Lal: "Don't be too hard on him. Send him here and I'll fix him."

Mr. Gupta: "I too have been making it with the maid and have the same symptoms."

Dr. Lal: "Then come over along with your son."

Mr. Gupta: "I think I have given the infection to my wife too."

"Oh no!" roared Dr. Lal. "That means we have all got it."

Observation by American Medical Association:

Over the past few years more and more money has been spent on breast implants and sildenafil (Viagara) than is spent on Alzheimer's disease research. It is now projected that by the year 2015, there will be 50 million people wandering around with huge breasts and erections who can't remember what to do with them!

A little boy asked his father:

"Papa what is sex?"

Being a doctor, the father thought that it was his duty to give him an explanation and proceeded to do so.

"But how am I going to fit all this in the little box here?" asked the boy holding up a form, in which he had to enter his

Name

Age

Sex

Address etc.

To stop her five years old daughter from sucking her thumb her mother frightened her:

"If you don't stop this habit, your stomach will swell up and finally burst one fine day."

This alarmed the little girl and she gave up the habit. A few days later her pregnant aunt came to visit them. Little girl looked at her aunt's bloated tummy and declared:

"I know exactly what you have been up to!"

First honeymoon - Agra

Second honeymoon - Viagra!

After a heart operation the cardiologist asked the patient to take it easy for a couple of months.

Patient: "What about sex?"

Doctor: "Only with your wife. Too much excitement is not good for you."

A doctor gave Viagra tablets to a middle aged man with sexual problems and advised him to take it ½ an hour before the act.

"It will take me precisely that much time to reach home." said the man popping the tablet in his mouth.

To his dismay he learnt that his wife was not at home.

He rang up the doctor to find a way out of his predicament.

"Make do with the maid." advised the doctor.

"But I don't need Viagra with my maid!"

A newly graduated doctor presented a tablet of Viagra to his grandfather on his fiftieth marriage anniversary and said:

"Take it before bedtime. If you like it put Rs500/- under my pillow."

The next day the lad was surprised to find Rs1500/- under his pillow.

"Thanks for your generosity grandpa." said the boy.

"Well I put just Rs500, the rest came from your grandmother!"

A box of Viagra was stolen from a medical store. The police are now on the lookout for 'hardened' criminals!

A man told his doctor that he is unable to sustain an errection.

Doc: "Are you married."

Man: "No."

Doc: "Do you have a girlfriend?"

Man: "No."

Doc: "Do you masturbate?"

Man: "No."

Doc: "Then what do you want an erection for? To hang a calendar?"

The Doctor & Other Professionals

A veterinarian was feeling ill and went to see her doctor. The doctor was taking a detailed history of her symptoms when she interrupted him: "Hey look, I'm a vet — I don't need to ask my patients questions: I can tell what's wrong just by looking. Why can't you?"

The doctor nodded, looked her up and down and handing her a prescription and said, "There you are. Of course, if *hat* doesn't work, we'll have to have you put down."

Doctor to his car mechanic: "How come You charge several times more than me per hour?"

"Doc, you've had the same model since Adam and Eve. I have to deal with new models every year."

Annoyed by the people who discussed medical problems at social gatherings, a doctor asked a lawyer friend:

"Should I send a bill to that obnoxious lady who talked at length about her piles at dinner?"

"Why not? After all she has taken medical advice from you."

The next day he received a bill from the lawyer 'for legal services rendered'.

A waiter went to the hospital for a surgery. He lay on the operation table but doctor after doctor went past, ignoring him altogether.

"Will someone please attend to me?" he implored.

"Sorry," said a passing surgeon "Not my table."

An auto-rickshaw driver lay on the table for an operation on his leg. To his alarm the surgeon began preparing his arm for surgery.

But, but," stammered the hapless patient, "I have a problem in my leg not arm."

"So what?" answered the surgeon "When I want to got to Patel Nagar you say 'Subzi Mandi *chalna hai toan chalo.*'

A doctor called a plumber to his house to repair a burst pipe. The plumber repaired the fault and handed the doctor a bill of Rs. 1000.

“This is ridiculous!” exclaimed the doctor. “I don’t charge this much for a house visit.”

“Neither did I when I was a doctor.” replied the plumber quietly.

A cardiac surgeon took his car to a mechanic for repair. The mechanic grumbled:

"What's the difference between your job and mine?

I too remove old values from the engine and put in new ones, like you do with human hearts. How come you get paid so much more?"

"Try doing it with a running engine!" said the surgeon.

When his auto mechanic came in for an operation, his surgeon took the opportunity to turn the tables on him.

“Well Mister,” said the doctor, “It’s going to take at least five days for the parts to get in. As for the cost, there’s no way to tell until we get in there and see exactly what the problem is.”

An ophthalmologist cured a famous painter of his cataract. In gratitude the good fellow painted a portrait of the doctor in the pupil of an eye and presented it to him. The doctor shuddered to think what he would paint when his wife, an obstetrician, delivered the artist's wife!

A doctor told a woman that she has only six more months to live.

"Whatever shall I do?" exclaimed the woman wringing her hands.

"Marry an accountant." said the doctor.

"Will that make me live longer?"

"No," replied the doctor. "But it will seem longer."

The Family Physician

A patient rang up a doctor at 2 am and asked:

"What are your fees at the clinic?"

"Rs 50/-."

"And how much do you take for a home visit?"

"Rs 200/-"

"In that case we'll meet at the clinic in half an hour."

A doctor came out of the examination room and began to write a prescription. A nurse said, "Excuse me, Doctor, but you are trying to write with your thermometer." The doctor looked at the thermometer and said, "God! Where did I leave my pen?

The family physician went on a vacation, entrusting his practice to his son. When the old man returned, the young doctor told his father that he had cured the wealthy old widow, Mrs. Puri, of her indigestion.

"My boy, it was Mrs. Puri's indigestion that put you through college."

A government employee went to his GP complaining of fatigue and weakness. The doctor examined him and said: "You need rest. Join duty at once."

A man went to a doctor seeking a cure for his insomnia.

"If you want to sleep well, do not take your troubles to bed with you." Said the doctor.

"I can't do that. My wife refuses to sleep in another room." replied the hapless man.

A young woman went to her doctor and said:

"You have to help me, I hurt all over".

"What do you mean, all over?" asked the doctor, "Be a little more specific."

The woman touched her right knee with her index finger and yelled, "Ouch! That hurts."

Then she touched her left cheek and again yelled, "That hurts, too." Then she touched her right earlobe, "Ow, even THAT hurts".

The doctor looked at her thoughtfully for a moment and said, "You have a broken finger."

A guy walked into work, and both his ears bandaged up. The boss asked, "What happened to your ears?"

"Yesterday I was ironing a shirt when the phone rang and I accidentally answered the iron."

"That explains one ear, but what happened to your other ear?"

"Well, I had to call the doctor!"

A man went to the doctor and said, "Doc, I would like to live very long. What should I do?"

"I think that is a wise decision," the doctor replies. "Let's see, do you smoke?"

"Half a pack a day."

"Starting NOW, no more smoking."

The man agreed.

The doctor then asked, "Do you drink?"

"Oh, well Doc, not much, just a bit of wine with my meals, and a beer or two every once in a while."

"Starting now, you drink only water. No exceptions."

The man got a bit upset, but also agreed to this.

The doctor asked, "What do you eat?"

"Oh, well, you know, Doc, normal stuff."

"Starting now you are going on a very strict diet."

The man was really worried.

"Doc, is all this really necessary?"

"Do you want to live long?"

"Yes."

"Then don't even think of breaking the diet.

"The man appeared agitated but asked the doctor to continue.

"Do you have sex?"

"Once a week or so... only with my wife!" he added hurriedly.

"No more sex for you."

The man was appalled. "Doctor are you sure I'm going to live longer this way?"

"I have no idea, but however long you live, I assure you, it will seem like an eternity!"

A woman who had been presecribed testosterone returned for a follow-up visit. Worried about the side effects she said:

"Doctor, the hormones you presecribed have helped

but I think the dose is rather high. I've started growing hair in places that I've never grown hair before."

The doctor reassured her. "A little hair growth is a known side-effect of testosterone. Just where has this hair appeared?"

"On my balls."

A man went to the doctor with a long history of migraine headaches. The poor fellow had taken practically every therapy known to man for his migraines and still there was no improvement.

"Listen," says the Doc, "I have migraines too and the advice I'm going to give you isn't really anything I learned in medical school, but something that I've gotten from my own experience. When I have a migraine, I go home, get in a nice hot bathtub, and soak for a while. Then I have my wife sponge me off with the hottest water I can stand, especially around the forehead. This helps a little. Then I get out of the tub, take her into the bedroom, and even if my head is killing me, I force myself to have intercourse with her. Almost always, the headache is immediately gone. Now, give it a try, and come back and see me in six weeks."

Six weeks later, the patient returned with a huge grin. "Doc! I took your advice and it really works! I've had migraines for 17 years and this is the 1st time anyone has ever helped me!"

"Well," said the physician, "I'm glad I could help."

"By the way, Doc," added the patient, "You have a lovely house."

A man went to a doctor, complaining that he hadn't been feeling very well.

After examining him, the doctor left the room and returned with three different bottles of pills.

"Take one blue pill with a large glass of water when you wake up in the morning. After lunch, take one red pill with a large glass of water. Then, just before going to bed, take one green pill with a large glass of water,".

"Gosh, doc, that sure is a lot of medication," "What's wrong with me?"

"You aren't drinking enough water!" replied the doctor.

A seventy-two-year-old man went to a doctor for a general checkup. After exhaustive lab tests, the doctor said that he was doing "fairly well" for his age.

A little concerned, the old man asked the doctor, "Do you think I'll live to be 90?"

The doctor asked, "Well, do you smoke or drink beer?"

"Oh no, I've never done either."

"Do you eat mutton?"

"No, I've know that red meat is not good for health."

"Do you spend a lot of time in the sun?" the doctor asked.

"No, I don't,"

Then the doctor asked, "Do you gamble, drive fast cars, or run around with sexy women?"

"No, I don't do any of those things."

The good doctor looked at man and asked, "Then why the heck do you want to live to be 90?"

Part II
Specialists

You Might Be A Casuality Medical Officer if...

· Your favorite hallucinogen is exhaustion.

· Discussing dismemberment over a gourmet meal seems perfectly normal to you.

· You think that caffeine should be available in IV form.

· You get an almost irresistible urge to stand and wolf your food even in the nicest restaurants.

· You believe that the waiting room should be equipped with a Valium fountain.

· You say to yourself "great veins" when looking at complete strangers.

· You believe that unspeakable evils will befall you if anyone says, "Boy it is quiet around here."

· You have ever referred to someone's death as a transfer to the "Eternal Care Unit".

- You have ever had a patient say, "I swear I never did anything. How can I be pregnant?"

- Your idea of fine dining is anywhere you can sit down to eat.

- You have ever had a patient look you straight in the eye and say "I have no idea how that got stuck in there".

- Your most common assessment question is "What changed tonight to make it an emergency after 6 (hours, days, weeks, months, years)?"

Multispeciality

The New Hospital Wing

When a panel of doctors was asked to vote on adding a new wing to their hospital, the Allergists voted to scratch it and the Dermatologists advised against rash moves.

The Gastroenterologists had a gut feeling about it, but the Neurologists thought the administration had a lot of nerve, and the Obstetricians stated they were all labouring under a misconception.

The Ophthalmologists considered the idea short-sighted, the Pathologists yelled, "Over my dead body", while the Pediatricians said,"Grow up!"

The Psychiatrists thought the whole idea was madness, the surgeons decided to wash their hands of the whole thing and the Radiologists could see right through it!

The physicians thought it was a bitter pill to swallow, and the Plastic Surgeons said, "This puts a whole new face on the matter."

The Podiatrists thought it was a step forward, but the Urologists felt the scheme wouldn't hold water. The Anesthesiologists thought the whole idea was gas and the Cardiologist didn't have the heart to say no.

In the end, the Proctologists left the decision up to some butt hole in Administration.

Three doctors went duck hunting and a bird flew overhead. The general practitioner looked at it and said, "Looks like a duck, flies like a duck... it's probably a duck," He took a shot at it but missed and the bird flew away.

When the next bird came into view, the pathologist looked at it, then through the pages of a bird manual, and said, "Hmmmm...white wings, yellow bill, quacking sound...might be a duck." By the time he raised his gun to shoot, the bird was long gone.

The surgeon raised his gun and shot down a third bird almost without looking, then turned to the pathologist and said, "Go see if that was a duck."

Two doctors, a psychiatrist and a protocologist, opened an office in a small town and put up a sign "Hysterias and Posteriors."

The town council was not happy with the sign, so the doctors changed it to "Minds and Behinds." still no good.

Another attempt resulted in "Lost Souls and Butt Holes." Unacceptable again!

so they tried "Nuts and Butts?" No way.

"Freaks and Cheeks?" Still no go.

"Loons and Moons?" Forget it.

Almost at their wit's end, the doctors finally came up with: "Odds and Ends."

Everyone loved it!

A radiologist, surgeon and physician went to God to ask for a boon.

Radiologist: "Dear God will there ever come a time when intervention therapy by radiologists would put surgeons out of business?"

"Not in your lifetime." Said God

Physician: "God will there ever come a time when I would be able to prevent all diseases by gene therapy?"

God: "Not in your life time."

Surgeon" "God will I ever be as intelligent as a physician?"

God: "Not in my lifetime."

Q. How many GPs does it take to change a light bulb?

A. (i) None - they just tell it to take two aspirins and come later.

(ii) One, but he has to have a nurse to tell him which end to screw in.

(iii) Three - one to find a bulb specialist, one to find a bulb installation specialist, and one to bill it all to Medicare.

Q. How many surgeons does it take to change a light bulb?

A. None. They would wait for a suitable donor and do a filament transplant.

Q. How many veterinarians does it take to change a light bulb?

A. Three. One to change the bulb and two to complain that an MD makes ten times as much for the same procedure!!

Q. How many physiotherapists does it take to change a light bulb?

A. None. They just give the dead bulb some exercises to do and hope it will be working a bit better the next time they see it.

Surgery

Things You Don't Want to Hear During Surgery

- Has anyone seen my watch?
- That was some party last night. I can't remember when I've been that drunk.
- Damn! Page 47 of the manual is missing!
- Well this book doesn't say that... What edition is your manual?
- Okay, now take a picture from this angle. This is truly a freak of nature.
- Better save that. We'll need it for the autopsy.
- Come back with that! Bad Dog!
- Wait a minute; if this is his spleen, then what was that?
- Hand me that... uh... that uh... thingie...

- Hey, has anyone ever survived 500 ml of this stuff before?
- Damn, there go the lights again...
- There's big money in kidneys and the guy's got two of them.
- Everybody stand back! I lost my contact lens!
- Could you stop that thing from beating; it's throwing my concentration off.
- I wish I hadn't forgotten my glasses.
- Well folks, this will be an experiment for all of us.
- Oops! It fell down. The floor's clean, right?
- This patient has already had some kids, am I correct?
- Nurse, did this patient sign the organ donation card?
- Don't worry. I think it is sharp enough.
- I don't know what it is, but hurry up and pack it in ice.
- Let's hurry, I don't want to miss "Bay Watch"
- That laughing gas stuff is pretty cool. Can I have some more of that?
- Hey Charlie, unzip the bag on that one, he's still moving.
- Of course I've performed this operation before, Nurse!

- This guy used to beat me up in school! I'll show hir
- Don't worry it probably won't happen to this one tc
- Let's cut this, just for fun.
- FIRE! FIRE! Everyone get out!

Four surgeons were taking a coffee break ar discussing their work. The first surgeon said, "I think th accountants are the easiest to operate on. You open ther up and everything inside is numbered."

The second surgeon said, "I think that librarians are th easiest to operate on. You open them up and everything i in alphabetical order."

The third surgeon said, "I think that electricians are th easiest to operate on. You open them up and everything i color coded."

The fourth surgeon said, "I think that lawyers are the easie to operate on. They're heartless, spineless, gutless, ar the head and butt are interchangeable."

A surgeon was about to operate upon his father. T fearful parent said:

"Son, think of it this way… if anything happens to r your mother is coming to live with you."

Apprehensive of an impending operation, a young boy clutched the surgeon's arm and asked

"Doctor, doctor will I die?"

"Yes my son and so will I."

A man walked into a surgeon's office and said

"I want to be castrated."

"What on earth for?" asked the doctor in amazement.

"It's something I've been thinking about for a long time and I want to have it done"

"But have you thought it through properly?" asked the doctor, "It's a very serious operation and once it's done, there's no going back. It will change your life forever!"

"I'm aware of that and you're not going to change my mind - either you book me in to be castrated or I'll simply go to another doctor."

"Well, OK." said the doctor, "But it's against my better judgment!"

So the man had his operation, and the next day he was up and walking very slowly, legs apart, down the hospital corridor with his drip stand. Heading towards him was another patient, who was walking exactly the same way.

"It looks as if you've just had the same operation as me."

"Well," said the other patient, "I finally decided after 37 years that I would like to be circumcised."

The castrated man stared at him in horror and screamed, "Shit! THAT'S the word!"

A surgeon to a patient in the immediate postoperative period

"I'm afraid that we'll have to open you up again. I have left a towel inside your body by mistake."

Patient: "I'd rather pay for the towel than undergo a repeat surgery!"

Neurosurgeon to nurse: "See to it that this patient does not disappear. He has been admitted thrice before for brain surgery and ran away after a hair cut." The desperation of recession!

A surgeon was performing an operation on an elephant. Towards the end the nurse did a quick instrument and swab count and then asked perplexed: "But where is the surgeon?"

A man was apprehensive before his surgery and his doctor was trying to allay his fears.

"What is there to worry about?"

"But doctor it is my first operation?

"So? It is my first too and I am not a bit nervous."

Question: How do you hide a thousand rupee note from surgeons?

Answer: Keep it in the case file. They rarely open it.

A middle-aged woman had a heart attack and was taken to the hospital. While on the operating table she had a near death experience. Seeing God she asked "Is my time up?"

God answered, "No, you have another 40 years, 2 months and 8 days to live."

After recovery, she decided to stay in the hospital and have a facelift, liposuction, and a tummy tuck. She even had someone come in and change her hair color. Since she had so much more time to live, she figured she might as well make the most of it.

After her last operation, she was released from the hospital. While crossing the street on her way home, she was hit by a car and died immediately.

Arriving in front of God, she demanded, "I thought you said I had another 40 years, why didn't you pull me from out of the path of the car?"

God: "I didn't recognize you."

After a long and complicated, a patient complained of a horrible headache and a lump on his head. Since his surgery had been an intestinal one, the nurse couldn't understand why he would be complaining about an aching head. Fearing that perhaps he may be suffering from some form of post-surgery shock, she decided to ask a surgeon about it.

"There's nothing to worry about, nurse," explained the surgeon. "He actually does have a bump on his head. Halfway through the operation we ran out of anesthetic."

Two carrots were walking down the street when one was run over by a cycle. The other carrot took his squashed friend to the hospital and waited on tenterhooks till the doctor performed a difficult surgery.

"How is my friend?" he asked anxiously as the surgeon emerged from the OT.

"We have been able to save him but he will remain a vegetable for the rest of his life."

A surgeon with precious little surgical skill removed everything from the pelvis of a woman except the hospital scissors. As expected the woman died after a stormy postoperative period. The husband, an honest fellow (and the delight of every doctor in this era of litigation), retrieved the scissors from her ashes cleaned and wrapped it a towel and returned the hospital property to the doctor!

A surgeon went to visit his twin brother, a vicar, at a parish. During his morning walk a parishioner, mistaking him for the vicar, congratulated him on his sermon.

"Sorry," replied the surgeon "I am not the twin who preaches, I am the one who practices."

A young woman with purple hair, sporting a variety of tattoos, and wearing strange clothing, was wheeled into the emergency room. It was quickly determined that she had acute appendicitis and was scheduled for immediate surgery. When she was completely disrobed on the operating table, the staff noticed that her pubic hair had been dyed green, and above it there was a tattoo that read, "Keep off the grass."

Once the surgery was completed, the surgeon wrote a short note on the patient's dressing, which said,

"Sorry, had to mow the lawn."

A man had terrible headaches. He couldn't sleep, eat, think, or do much of anything because of the pain. Several doctors examined him and couldn't determine the cause of his problem. He finally went to one of the top neurological specialists in the country who said, "I've found the cause of the pain. Your testicles are pushing up into your spine. The constant pressure on the spine causes the headaches. The only thing I can do is perform surgery and remove your testicles."

The man was shocked to hear this but decided to go in for the operation, as he could not stand the pain. He had the surgery and immediately felt like a new man. The pain was completely gone. Overjoyed, he decided to give himself a treat. He went to a tailor and said that he wanted to buy a suit.

"Sure," said the tailor. "You're a 42 length, right?"

"Wow, how did you know?" says the man.

"Hey, I've been in this business a long time. You learn a few things." said the tailor.

The tailor brought the man a suit that fit perfectly. It looked so good that the man decided to buy a new shirt to go with it.

"16, 34, right?" said the tailor.

"Right again!" said the man. "You're amazing."

"Hey, I've been in this business a long time. You learn a few things".

The tailor brought a shirt and tie and they looked great. The man said, "Hey, give me a pair of the silk boxers too."

The tailor said, "36 right?"

"I'm disappointed," said the man. "But 2 out of 3 is still good. I wear size 34 boxers."

The tailor said, "Hey, I've been in this business for a long time and I think you need 36."

The man replied, "It's obvious you know your business but I've worn size 34 for as long as I can remember. I'm going to have to disagree with you on this one".

"Hey look," said the tailor, "I'll sell you whatever you want. But I've been in this business a long time. If you wear a size 34 it's going to push your nuts up into your spine and give you terrible headaches.

Transplants

While performing a vasectomy, the doctor accidentally cut off one of the man's testicles. In order to avoid a huge malpractice suit, the doctor replaced the missing testicle with an onion.

A few weeks later, the man returned to the doctor for a check-up.

"How's your sex life?" asked the doctor.

"Pretty good," the man replied, "but I have been having some strange side effects."

"Such as?" asked the doctor asked nervously.

"Well, every time I piss my eyes water," explained the man. "When my wife gives me a blow job, she gets heartburn, and every time I pass a hot dog stand, I get a hard-on."

A villager's penis was amputated in an accident. The surgeon replaced it by the trunk of a baby elephant and asked him to come for a follow up after a couple of months.

"How are you doing?" asked the doctor.

"Everything else is fine except for one problem."

"And what is that?"

"Each time I go to the fields to relieve myself it breaks off sugarcane shoots and shoves them up my behind!"

A team of doctors was busy performing a kidney transplant. They took out the kidney from the donor and were opening up the recipient when to their horror a cat came in and ate up the donor kidney. Even as they were wondering what to do a junior came up with a brilliant idea. They took out the kidney of their pet dog and transplanted it.

When the patient came for a follow up after a month the doctor asked how he was faring.

"Everything is fine except for the fact that ever time I want to pass urine I get an irresistible age to lift one leg!"

A man, needing a heart transplant was told by his doctor that, the only heart available was that of a sheep. The man agreed and the doctor transplanted the sheep heart into the man. A few days after the operation, the man came for a checkup and the doctor asked him "How are you feeling?" The man replied "Not BAAAAD!"

A patient needed a brain transplant for an inoperable brain tumour. The doctor offered him a choice of available brains.

"You could have a doctor's brain. It is for Rs. 100,000.

"That would be nice but what else do you have?"

"A genius scientist's brain - for Rs.250,000 lacs."

"Wonderful but money is no problem. Show me the best you have."

"Well it's a politician's brain. It is for 100,00,000."

"One corore rupees for a politician's brain! Why is it so expensive?"

"Because it has never been used."

Paediatrics

While visiting a hospital I overheard a proud young mother, 'Look at that," she said "Only two days old and already he is just like his father. He sleeps while I talk with him."

Mrs. Rita: "Doctor, my son believes in Preventive Medicine."

Dr. Lal: "That's wonderful."

Rita: "You don't understand Doctor he tries to prevent me from giving him medicine."

A doctor tried to play a game with his little patient, to test his knowledge about body parts. He pointed to the boy's ear and asked:

"Is that your nose?"

The boy turned to his mother and said:

"I think we better find a new doctor!"

"Will someone please help?" screamed a woman at a party. "My son has swallowed a coin."

A man got up from the adjoining table walked nonchalantly up to the boy and squeezed his balls. Out popped the coin.

"Thank you sir. Are you are a doctor?"

"No. I am from the income tax department."

"I don't understand doctor," a boy asked his doctor. "When I stand on my head all the blood rushes to it. Why doesn't that happen when I stand on my feet?"

"That is because you feet aren't empty!" replied the doctor.

A woman thought that the doctor had overcharged her for treating her son's measles and told him so.

"Don't forget that I made four house calls." The doctor reminded her.

"And you don't forget that my son infected the entire school."

Two sick children were talking to each other in the children's ward.

"Are you a medical case or a surgical one?" asked one boy.

"I don't understand what do you mean?"

"Were you sick before you came to the hospital or after?"

Two young boys are lying on stretchers next to each other outside the operating room.

The first boy asks, "What are you in here for?"

"I'm getting my tonsils out and I'm kind of nervous," replied the second boy.

"You've got nothing to worry about," said the first boy. "I had that done when I was five. They put you to sleep and when you wake up, they give you lots of jelly and ice cream."

"What are you in for?" asks the second boy

"I'm going to be circumcised."

"I had that done when I was born and couldn't walk for a year!"

Obstetrics & Gynaeocology

A gynecologist is one who looks for problems in a place, where others look for pleasure.

Gynecology is the best profession. Where else can you tell a woman to take off her panties, touch her breasts, insert your finger in her and ask her husband to pay for it!"

Maternity is a fact, paternity an opinion.

Sign in a hospital – NO CHILDREN ALLOWED IN MATERNITY WARDS.

IF MEN GOT PREGNANT.....

- Maternity leave would last for two years - with full pay.
- Morning sickness would become number one health problem.

- There'd be a cure for stretch marks.
- They'd stay in bed for the entire nine months.
- Natural childbirth would become obsolete.
- A birth-control method with 100% effectiveness would be discovered.
- Children would be kept in the hospital till they were toilet-trained.
- Men would be eager to talk about commitment.
- They wouldn't think twins were quite so cute.
- Fathers would insist that their sons be home by 10 PM.
- Men would use their briefcases as diaper bags.
- Paternity suits will be a line of clothes.
- WOMEN WOULD RULE THE WORLD.

The wife of an obstetrician to a flirtatious patient of his: "My husband delivers babies. He does not install them."

Patient: "Doctor, I've had six abortions when I was unmarried but ever since I have tied the knot I am unable to conceive."

Obstetrician: "Evidently you do not breed in captivity."

Q. Should I have a baby after 35?

A. No 35 children are more than enough.

Q. I am three months pregnant, when will the baby move?

A. With luck, after he finishes college.

Q. What is the most common craving during pregnancy?

A. Men aught to be the ones who got pregnant.

Q. What is the most reliable method to determine the sex of the child?

A. Childbirth.

Q. My childbirth instructor says that it is not pain you feel during labour but pressure.

A. In quite the same way a tornado can be called an air current.

Q. When is the best time to get an epidural?

A. Soon after you discover that you are pregnant?

Q. Does pregnancy cause piles?

A. It causes anything you want to blame it for.

Q. Our baby was born last week. When will my wife begin to feel and act normal again?

A. When the kids are in college.

Q. What is the best time for weaning a baby?

A. When you see teeth marks.

Q. My wife is five months pregnant and very moody.

A. So what's your question?

Q. The more obviously pregnant I get, the more people smile at me. Why?

A. Because you are getting fatter than more and more people.

A woman goes to her doctor who verifies that she is pregnant. As it is her first time, she is worried and asks her doctor: "How much will childbirth hurt?"

The doctor answered, “Well, that varies from woman to woman and pregnancy to pregnancy and besides, it’s difficult to describe pain.”

“I know, but can’t you give me some idea?” she asked.

“Grab your upper lip and pull it out a little...”

“Like this?”

“A little more...”

“Like this?”

“No. A little more...”

“Like this?”

“Yes. Does that hurt?”

“A little bit.”

“Now stretch it over your head.”

A man spoke frantically into the phone, “My wife is pregnant, and her contractions are only two minutes apart!”

“Is this her first child?” asked the doctor.

“No, you *idiot*!” “This is her *husband*!”

A doctor was called to deliver a woman at home. A little while later he put his head out and asked:

"Have you got a screw driver?" He was handed one instantly.

After a while, he asked for a hammer and later on for a saw. By this time the husband was in cold sweat.

"Is the labour very difficult? He asked anxiously.

"I don't know about the labour. I am still trying to open my bag!"

Patient: "Is the doctor in?"

Servant: "No.".

Patient: "When is he expected back?"

Servant: "I don't know sir. He has gone out for an eternity case."

A doctor was called to a remote village to deliver a child. When he reached the cottage he was surprised to find only her five years old son by her. Trying to make the best of the situation, he asked the little boy to hold the lantern while he delivered the baby. The boy watched avidly as the doctor held the newborn upside down and spanked his bottom to make him cry. Later, he asked the five year old what he though of his little brother.

"I think you should spank him again. He shouldn't have crawled in there in the first place."

A ninety years old millionaire married a twenty years old girl and went to the doctor to inform him that his wife was pregnant.

"Let me tell you a story," said the doctor. "An absentminded fellow went hunting carrying his umbrella in place of a gun. When a bear came charging, he pointed his umbrella towards the animal and killed it on the spot."

"Impossible!" exclaimed the old man, "Someone else must have shot the bear."

"Exactly." Replied the doctor.

A nurse came out of the labour room holding twins - one dark and one fair. Before she could announce the name of the father a man rushed forward to claim them.

"Are you Mr. Shyam?"

"Yes."

"How did you know that the babies were yours?"

"Well, my wife is typist so I assumed that the dark baby must be a carbon copy!"

A nurse came out of the labour room carrying a very dark baby. A man humbly assumed paternity of the child stating:

"My wife burns whatever she makes."

A villager was helping a midwife deliver his wife by holding aloft a kerosene lamp. When not one, not two but three babies emerged the farmer disappeared.

"Come back with the lamp at once." ordered the midwife. "I think that there is another baby."

"I will not. I think it is the light that is attracting them."

A man rang up the labour room to ask about his wife's progress. By mistake he was connected to the cricket stadium and this was the reply he got 'Two were out one after another and one after lunch break. By the way, the last one was a duck!'

A hugely pregnant woman boarded a bus and sat by the window. Soon after a young man got in, sat by her side, looked her up and down and started smiling. Embarrassed she got up and sat on the opposite seat, at which his smile widened into a grin. In exasperation she got up went further ahead and sat on a seat far removed from him. At this he burst into guffaws. Unable to bear it any longer she got up to confront him.

"Just what is it that amuses you? Surely your mother must have looked just like this when she was carrying you."

"Madam it's your choice of seats that amuse me. At first you sat under an advertisement that read '*hum do hamare do*'. As if this wasn't funny enough you got up and sat under 'Haldiram Bujia did the Magic' and what finally had me in splits was the last hoarding over your seat that read "Nirodh would have prevented the accident'."

I was sitting in the waiting room of the hospital after my wife had gone into labor when the nurse walked out and said to the man sitting next to me, "Congratulations sir, you're the new father of twins!"

The man replied, "How about that, I work for the Double mint Chewing Gum Company."

About an hour later, the same nurse entered the waiting room and announced that Mr. Smith's wife has just had triplets.

Mr. Smith stood up and said, "Well, how do you like that, I work for the 3M Company."

The gentleman sitting next to me got up to leave.

When I asked him why he was leaving, he remarked, "I think I need a breath of fresh air. I work for 7-UP."

Doctor husband to wife after the birth of their first child: "I am so broad minded that I am quite willing to have a vasectomy now."

"Go right ahead." said the wife, "I will have a tubectomy only after my third issue."

To her dismay a woman realised that she was pregnant for the fourth time. Furious with her husband she picked up the phone and berated him:

"How could you let this happen? As if all the other problems at home weren't enough, you had to make me pregnant! How will I ever manage? It's all your fault you asshole!!!"

There was silence at the other end.

"CAN YOU HEAR ME?" She screamed into the phone.

A barely audible whisper at the other end asked: "Who is this?"

Santa called up Domino's pizza for 'free home delivery' when his pregnant wife went into labour.

Fed up of child bearing, a delegation of women demanded a solution from the Almighty.

"As I cannot change your anatomy," said God, "I will arrange it so that you deliver the baby and the father of the child bears the pains.

Thanking Him happily the women returned to earth. When the first amongst them went into labour, strangely neither the woman nor her husband seemed to have any pain. Even as they were wondering what was happening they found the driver doubled over with pain in the car! Naturally the women rushed back and asked God to revert the boon as soon as possible!

An elderly woman told her doctor that she would like to have some birth control pills.

Surprised by her request, the doctor said to her, "Pardon me, but you're 78 years old. What possible use could you have for birth control pills?"

"They help me sleep doctor," she explained.

Now very confused, the doctor asked, "How would birth control pills help you to sleep?"

"Each morning I put one in my granddaughter's milk and I sleep much better at night," she replied.

A very fat lady had a problem with body odour, so she went to see her doctor.

"Do you wash?" the doctor asked her.

"Of course," she replied. "Every single morning I begin at my head and wash down as far as possible. Then, I begin at my feet and wash up as far as possible."

"Well," the doctor told her, "I suggest you go home and wash 'possible'."

A man from the census department asked Mrs. Lal how many children she had?

She said "There are the eldest twins Seeta and Geeta, the next set are Ram and Shyam, then came Antu and Montu and then…"

"Gosh!" said the census taker "You got twins every time?"

"Off course not! There were hundreds of times in between when we didn't get anything."

A news flash for women 'There is no need to fear menopause. It's the eggs that expire, not the hen !

"Why do women prefer old gynecologists?"
"Because they have shaky hands."

Psychiatry

Welcome to the Psychiatric Hotline.

- If you are obsessive compulsive please press 1 repeatedly.
- If you are co-dependent please ask someone to press 2.
- If you have a multiple personality disorder, please press 3, 4, 5 & 6.
- If you are paranoid-delusional, we know who you are and what you want. Please stay online so that we can trace the call.
- If you are schizophrenic, listen carefully and a little voice will tell you which number to press.
- If you are maniac-depressive it doesn't matter which number you press. No one will answer.
- If you are anxious, just start pressing numbers at random.

- If you are phobic don't press anything.
- If you are delusional and occasionally hallucinate, please beware that the thing you are holding on the side of your head is alive and is about to bite off your ear.
- If you do not know what your problem is wait for operator assistance.

How do two psychiatrists greet each other when they meet?

"Who am I?"

Two psychiatrists pass in the hall. The first one says "Hello."

The other thinks, "I wonder what he meant by that."

A psychiatrist met a friend and exclaimed, "I heard you died."

"But you see I'm alive," smiled the friend.

"Impossible," said the psychiatrist. "The man who told me is much more reliable than you."

Psychiatrist to his nurse: "Just say we're very busy. Don't keep saying 'It's a madhouse'."

A man told his psychiatrist that he had a split personality, so the doctor charged him double.

A man told his doctor that he forgets everything.

Doctor: "In that case, pay my bill in advance."

A psychotherapist wondered why he hardly got any patient after he had revamped his office and got a new board put up. People would stop outside his office, look at his board and hurry away.

Piqued he went out and read 'Psycho The Rapist'.

Why is psychoanalysis much quicker for men than it is for women?

Because when it is time to go back to childhood, the man is already there.

What is the difference between a psychiatrist and a psychologist?

If you say, "I hate my mother," the psychiatrist will ask:

"Why do you say that?"

While the psychologist will say:

"Thank you for sharing that with us."

Psychiatrist to patient:

"What is the difference between dream and reality?"

"The same between a girlfriend and wife."

"Doctor everybody thinks I am mad."

"But why?"

"Because I like omelets."

"There's nothing wrong with that. Why, even I like omelets."

"Really?" said the man excitedly, "Come I'll show you my collection."

Woman abashedly to a psychiatrist, "I think I am a nymphomaniac."

Psychiatrist, "I think I can help you but I charge Rs. 500 per hour.

Woman, "That's not too bad. How much do your charge for the entire night?"

A buxom young woman lay on her psychiatrist's couch telling him how frustrated she was since she always failed at everything she seemed to try.

"I've tried to be a secretary and failed," she complained. "I tried to be an actress and failed. Then, I tried sales and I failed at that too."

The doctor thought for a moment and then said, "It is important for everyone to live a full and meaningful life. Have you tried nursing?"

She looked down at her oversized breasts and said, "OK, I'll give it a try."

A psychiatrist was conducting a group therapy session with three young mothers and their small children. "You a' have obsessions," he observed.

To the first mother, he said, "You are obsessed with eatir

You've even named your daughter Candy."

He turned to the second mom. "Your obsession is money. It manifests itself in your child's name, Penny."

At this point, the third mother got up, took her little boy by the hand and whispered, "Come on, Dick, let's go."

A man was driving past a mental hospital when he noticed a puncture in his front, right hand tyre. He unscrewed the nuts and put them in the hub. Just then another vehicle went by, tipping the hub into a nearby pond. He was at a loss, as to what should be done when one of the inmates of the mental hospital called out:

"Take one nut off each of the remaining three tyres and put the stepnee. This will take you at least as far as the nearest mechanic.

"That was brilliant." said the stranded motorist, "How come they put you in here?"

"That's because I am crazy not stupid!"

Psychiatrist to a female patient:

"Congratulations! You are finally cured of thinking that you are someone else. But why are you sad?"

"Won't you feel sad if yesterday you were Cleopatra and the next day you are back to being nobody."

At a party the host asked a psychiatrist:

“How would you detect mental derangement in a seemingly normal patient?

"That's easy," said the shrink. "I ask him a simple question, which no normal person should have difficulty in answering.”

“Such as?”

“Mohammed Ghazni attacked India 16 times. During which attack did he die?”

“I am afraid my history is a little rusty. Could you ask another question?”

Psychiatrist to new patient:

“I would definitely like you to give up smoking before the next session.”

“Will that help me?” asked the patient eagerly.

“No but you will stop burning holes in my couch!”

A patient rushed to the doctor exclaiming:

“Doctor the voices I have been hearing in my brain for years have suddenly stopped.”

“Why, that is good news. So what is your problem?”

"I think I am going deaf."

A man visiting a psychiatrist for the first time was surprised when the learned doctor told him

"I see that you are an automobile mechanic."

"Your are wonderful doctor. I have not said a word and you already know what I do for a living."

"Its years of experience," said the shrink modestly. "Plus the fact that you are lying UNDER the couch."

A man walked up to the librarian and said, 'I borrowed a book last week but it was the most boring book I ever read. There was no story whatsoever and there were far too many numbers!'

The librarian replied. "Oh, you must be the lunatic who took our phone book!"

Patient to psychiatrist, "Doctor I am so ugly that I get depressed. I have no friends and everyone laughs at me. Please help me."

Psychiatrist, "I'll do my best. Now go and lie face down on the couch there."

A woman on therapy to her friend: "My therapist told me in order to achieve a sense of self-worth I should finish whatever I start so I finished two packets of chips and a box of chocolates and I am feeling better already.

A man came back from a visit to his psychiatrist raving and ranting.

"Can you imagine," he told his wife "The psychiatrist I have been seeing for the last 5 years, the one I told you, listened to my problems patiently without interrupting,"

"Well, what of him?"

"I have just learnt that he is deaf!"

A patient visited a doctor and complained that he couldn't sleep.

"The dogs in my street bark whole night keeping me awake."

"Don't worry," said the doctor "I'll help you solve your problem. Try these new sleeping pills and report to me a week later.

The patient returned after seven days looking more haggard than ever.

"The pills didn't work?" asked the doctor concerned.

"No." replied the hapless patient. "I have been chasing the dogs whole nights, night after night and even when I managed to catch one he wouldn't swallow the pill."

To a man obsessed with breast the psychiatrist said: "Let's play a little word association game. "I'll say a word and you say the first thing that comes to your mind."

"OK."

"Plums."

"Breasts."

"Oranges."

"Breasts."

"Watermelons."

"Breasts."

"Wipers."

"Breasts."

"I understand that plums, oranges, watermelons could remind you of breasts but wipers?" asked the baffled doctor.

"Easy," said the patient, "One on the right and one on the left."

A psychiatrist told his patient: “Let’s play a little game.”

“OK.”

He drew a triangle and asked: “What is this?”

“Sex.”

He then drew a small circle and asked: “And what is this?”

“Sex.”

“Two triangles.”

“Two people having sex.”

Doctor; “You are obsessed with sex.”

“You are the one drawing dirty diagrams, not me.”

There was a man who thought himself dead when he was very much alive. His frustrated family took him to a psychiatrist, who tired all the means at his disposal to convince the man that he was alive – and failed. Finally he asked the man:

“You do understand don’t you, that dead men do not bleed.”

“Yes I do.”

“Now I am going to perform a little experiment on you.”

He took a pin, pricked the man's finger and pointing to the drop of blood that welled, he asked:

"Now what do you make of this?"

"This is incredulous! Dead men *do* bleed!" replied the man.

A man walked into a psychiatrist's office, sat down, took out a pack of cigarettes. He removed a cigarette from the pack, unrolled it, and stuffed the tobacco up his nose. The shrink frowned and said, "I see you need my help!" The guy said, "Yeah, Doc. Got a match?"

A mental hospital short-listed two patients for release. To ensure that they were completely cured the authorities decided to ask them two questions. As the first one entered, the doctor asked:

"What would happen if I gouged out one eye of yours?"

"I'd become blind of one eye."

"What if your other eye too was gouged?"

"I'd become completely blind."

"Good. Now send the other patient in."

To help, his not-as-sane-as-him friend, the first one quickly told him what he was asked.

So when the second one was questioned:

"What will happen if I cut off your left ear?" he replied

"I'll become blind of one eye."

"And if I cut off the other ear?"

"I'll become totally blind?"

"How come?" asked the puzzled doctor.

"My specs will fall off!"

Three patients in a mental asylum were on their way to recovery. The psychiatrists decided to give them a final test before letting them loose into the world again. One by one, the three were taken to an empty swimming pool, made to climb up a diving board and asked to jump.

The first patient dived in and broke both his arms.

The second tried to land on his feet and broke both his legs.

The third refused to jump. Glad that at least one patient had passed the test the doctors congratulated him on his release and out of curiosity asked him why did he not jump.

"Well Doc, I can't swim."

After the new patient was comfortably ensconced on the couch, the psychiatrist asked him:

"Now begin at the beginning."

"In the beginning I created heaven and earth........."

A bald patient in a lunatic asylum went about wearing nothing but a loincloth. When asked why he did so, he replied:

"Because I am Mahatma Gandhi."

"How do you know?"

"God told me so."

At which, another patient loitering about burst forth:

"I certainly didn't!"

Two dogs were walking down the street. The Doberman said to the Dalmatian.

"My life is in a mess. My master is cruel. My mate is going around with an Alsatian. I am nothing but a loser."

"Why don't you see a psychiatrist?" suggested the Dalmatian.

"I can't because I am not allowed on the couch."

One patient in a mental asylum asked another:

"What are you carrying in that bag?"

"Chickens."

"If I guess how many are there will you let me have one?"

"You can have both."

"OK, I guess there are five."

Doctor to psychiatric patient:

If I lead a patient to a pail of water and a pail of beer which one will he drink?"

"Water."

"Why?"

"Because he is an ass."

A psychiatrist visited a mental institution and asked a patient, "How did you get in here?" and he got this reply...

"It all started when I got married and I guess I should never have done it. I got hitched to a widow with a grown daughter who then became my stepdaughter. My daddy came to visit us, fell in love with my lovely stepdaughter and married her. And so my stepdaughter was now my stepmother. Soon, my wife had a son who was, of course, my daddy's brother-in-law since he is the half-brother of my stepdaughter, who is now, of course, my daddy's wife. So, as I told you, when my stepdaughter married my daddy, she was at once my stepmother! Now, since my new son is brother to my stepmother, he also became my uncle. As you know, my wife is my step-grandmother since she is my stepmother's mother. Don't forget that my stepmother is my stepdaughter. Remember, too, that I am my wife's grandson. But hold on just a few minutes more. You see, since I'm married to my step-grandmother, I am not only the wife's grandson and her hubby, but I am also my own grandfather. Now can you understand how I got put in this place?"

Woman to psychiatrist, "My son is so naughty that he keeps me on tenterhooks whole day. What should I do?"

Doctor, "You worry too much about your son. Take tranquillizers daily."

On the next visit the psychiatrist asked, "Have the tranquillizers calmed you."

"They have worked very well."

"And how is your son?"

"Who cares?"

An old couple came out of a 'memory clinic' pleased with the therapy.

A friend asked the husband "How was it in there. Did your memory really improve?"

"O yes they used the latest technique to help us."

"What was the name of the clinic?"

"What is the name of the flower with a nice smell and thorns?"

"You mean a rose?"

Turning to his wife the man asked, "Rose do you remember the name of the clinic?"

Dentist

Lady to her dentist: "Its easier having a baby than getting a tooth removed."

"Decide quickly so that I know which end of the chair to raise."

When a dentist was caught raping a girl, a newspaper reported on the front page 'Dentist caught filling the wrong cavity.'

A dentist was about to extract the tooth of a lady when he pulled back in alarm.

"Madam you are holding my private parts." He exclaimed shocked.

"Yes I know doctor and we aren't going to hurt each other are we?"

A dentist was explaining the importance of dental floss to her young nephews and nieces.

"It's a pain in the ass." drawled a nephew.

"Which means that you're using it at the wrong end." retorted the aunt.

Boss angrily to secretary: "You took half day off because you had an appointment with your dentist."

"Yes Sir."

"Don't lie. I saw you come out of the theatre with a young man."

"He was my dentist."

A lady and her dentist had been carrying on a passionate affair in his dental clinic for many months. Finally he became a bit nervous about the whole situation and said to her, "Darling I think its best that we stop seeing each other. Your husband is bound to become suspicious."

"He is as dumb as a lamp post," she replied. "We've been carrying on for months now and he doesn't suspect a thing."

"That may be true, dear," the dentist, replied, "but you're down to your last tooth."

Patient: "How long will it take to pull out my tooth?"

Dentist: "Only two seconds"

Patient: "And how much will it cost?"

Dentist: "Rs 500."

Patient: "500 for a two seconds job!"

Dentist: "If you want I can pull it out slowly."

Ramesh: "Suresh, your father is a teacher and your sister does not know how to read a single letter."

"So what?" retorted Suresh. "Your father is a dentist and your little brother doesn't have single tooth!"

Dentist to Patient: "Would you help me out? I'd like you to give a few of your loudest screams."

Patient: "Why, Doc? I don't feel a thing!"

"You see I have got tickets for the nine o' clock show and my waiting room is full of patients."

"Open your mouth wide Mrs. Lal."

"Open your mouth wide Mrs. Lal." said the dentist.

"You have a very big cavity."

"You have a very big cavity." observed the dentist.

"Why do you repeat every sentence?" asked Mrs. Lal as soon as she could speak.

"I did not repeat a single word." replied the dentist. "The second time it was an echo."

A man with a painfully swollen mouth was asked by his dentist to open his mouth wider, wider.

Exasperated, the man asked:

"Do you intend sitting in my mouth to remove the tooth?"

A woman and her husband did not want to interrupt a long planned holiday on account of an urgent visit to the dentist.

"I want a tooth pulled out and I don't want local anesthesia because we are in a tearing hurry."

"Your certainly are a courageous woman!" exclaimed the dentist admiringly, "Which tooth is it?"

The woman turned to her husband and said "Show him your tooth dear."

ENT

Patient: “Doctor I have a speech impediment. Each time I open my mouth to speak my wife interrupts.”

At the doctor’s office a woman complained that she had been experiencing constant flatus. “Fortunately,” she added, “It doesn’t stink.”

The physician did his physical examination and instructed the woman “Take two of these pills tonight and call me in the morning.”

The woman did as told. In the morning, she discovered that her flatus continued, but now the odor was horrendous. She called him back.

“Well,” the doctor replied, “Now that your sinus problem is cured, let’s see what can be done about your flatulence.”

After reading a report in a journal, an ENT specialist learnt that chewing gum reduced the incidence of otitis media by 30-40%. He gave the information to the mother of a little boy who had middle ear infection. The next day she brought him to the office - his ear plugged with chewing gum!

Towards the end of his life, W.C. fields, the great comic and tippler was advised by his doctor to stop drinking lest he lose his hearing. He did not heed his doctor's advice because, as he told a friend:

"The stuff I've been drinking is so much better than the stuff I've been hearing!"

A rich gentleman was having hearing problems for quite some time. One day he went to the ENT specialist and got himself fitted with a hearing aid. When he returned after a month for follow up the doctor remarked:

"Your family must be happy that you have started hearing again."

"I haven't told my family yet. I just sit quietly listening to their conversations. It has made me change my will three times."

An old man told the doctor that his wife was getting deaf.

"How bad is it?" asked the doctor."

"I can't say exactly."

"You could test her standing at a distance of 20' and asking her a question. If she does not answer keep coming closer and repeat the same question till she answers."

So the man stood 20' away and asked her:

"What are we having for dinner?"

When he got no answer he repeated the same question from a distance of 15' and 10' with no reply. When he was within 5' feet, he asked her again:

"What are we having for dinner?"

She turned around and said: "This is the fourth time I am telling you it is rice and chicken."

Doctor, how do I stop my nose from running?

Stick your foot out and trip it.

Opthalmology

Patient to the eye doctor: "Whenever I drink coffee, I have this sharp pain in my eye."

"Try removing the spoon from the cup before drinking."

Doctor: "You need glasses."

Patient: "I am already wearing glasses."

Doctor: "Then I need glasses."

Doc: "We've managed to save one of your eyes."

Patient: "Thank you very much Doc."

Doc: "We'll give it to you on your way out."

"Doctor I think I need glasses."

"You certainly do Sir this is a Pizza Hut!!"

Patient: "I see spots before my eyes."

Doctor: "Didn't the new glasses help?"

Patient: "Sure, I now see the spots better."

Patient: "I see spots in front of my eyes."

Receptionist "Have you ever seen a doctor?"

Patient: "No, just spots."

A woman rushed into an office and asked:

"Doctor what is wrong with me."

He eyed her from top to toe and said:

"For one thing you are too fat. For another you use too much eye shadow. Your breath smells and one more thing."

"What?" asked the stunned woman.

"You cannot read."

"What do you mean?"

"This is a bookstore, not a doctor's office."

As soon as she entered the doctor's office a woman began rattling:

"Doctor when I woke up this morning, I looked at myself in the mirror and saw my hair all wiry and frazzled up, my skin all wrinkled and pasty, my eyes blood-shot and bulging out, and I had this corpse-like look on my face! What's wrong with me?"

The doctor looked her over for a couple of minutes and calmly stated, "All, I can for sure is that there is nothing wrong with your eyesight."

A man went to an eye specialist to get his eyes tested and asked, "Doctor, will I be able to read after wearing glasses?"

"Why not?" replied the doctor

"That's wonderful, I have never learnt to read."

An optometrist was instructing a new employee on how to charge a customer: "If he asks how much they cost, you say Rs1000...' If he doesn't blink, say, 'For the frames. The lenses will be an additional Rs1000...' If he still doesn't blink, you add '...Each.'"

A man went to an ophthalmologist complaining of double vision.

"But why have both of you come together?" asked the doctor.

Optician: "I have made three pairs of specs for you; one for distant vision and one for near vision…."

"And the third?" asked the anxious patient.

"For seeing where you have kept the other two."

Doctor: "How many fingers are these?"

Patient: "Thirteen."

Doctor: "I do not know if something is wrong with your eyes or with your arithmetic."

Prof: "What increases by many times its original size during excitement?"

The student blushed and could only stammer an incoherent answer.

Prof: "The pupil"

Chest Specialist

Doctor: "Your cough sounds a lot better."

Patient: "It should. I have been practicing all night."

A doctor asked a patient with chest infection:

"Is there any coughing, wheezing or shortness of cash?"

Notice in the office of a chest specialist who enjoyed smoking – DO AS I SAY, NOT AS I DO.

Patient: "I once heard of a doctor who treated a patient for pneumonia who finally died of typhoid."

Doctor: "Don't worry, it won't happen with you. If I treat someone for pneumonia, he dies of pneumonia."

A junior doctor was examining his first patient. After a while he asked the patient to cough.

"But I can't doctor." said the patient.

"Try." cajoled the doctor.

"I really can't, my throat hurts."

"I'll thump you on the back to help you." and he slammed his fist on the patient's back.

To escape further 'help' the poor fellow gave a feeble cough.

"Now mister," said the young doctor confidently "How long have you had this cough?"

A man with pneumonia rang up the hospital to fix an appointment with the chest specialist.

"Come after three weeks." said the secretary.

"But I'll be dead by then."

"In that case tell your wife to call up and cancel the appointment.

A man went to see his doctor because he was suffering from a miserable cold. His doctor prescribed some pills, but they didn't help.

On his next visit the doctor gave him a shot, but that didn't do any good.

On his third visit the doctor told the man, "Go home and take a hot bath. As soon as you finish bathing throw open all the windows and stand in the draft."

"But doc," protested the patient, "If I do that, I'll get pneumonia."

"I know," said the doctor, "I can cure pneumonia."

Orthopaedics

An old lady went to the doctor complaining of pain in her right knee. The orthopedic specialist prescribed some medicine and told her that her problem was due to old age.

"What nonsense!" exclaimed the old lady, "My left knee is as old as my right knee and there is nothing wrong with it."

A lady went skiing downhill felt the urge to urinate.

With no washroom facilities nearby, she found a sheltered area, dropped her pants and proceeded to relieve herself.

Suddenly she found herself beginning to slide backwards, out into the open and down the slope with her pants around her knees. She crashed and broke her leg.

The paramedics rushed her to the local hospital. A doctor came in to examine her, laughing hysterically. "You're not going to believe this," he said, "But the guy in the next room claims he fell off the ski lift and broke his leg because he saw a naked lady skiing backwards down the mountain!"

He then composed himself and asked the lady, "So, how did you break YOUR leg??"

After a knee joint replacement the doctor told the patient:

"You will need a walker for some time."

"Will Johnny Walker do?"

What is a double blind study?

Two orthopedics, reading an ECG

An orthopedic professor asked his resident to get the knees of a particularly unattractive woman X rayed. A while later the professor enquired whether the job was done.

"Yes Sir *bhoothnee ke* X Rays *karva diye hain.*"

"How dare you call my wife a *bhoothnee*!" said the professor,

"But sir, I just said 'both knees' *ke* X Rays…"

An old man had a knee replacement one year. This was followed by a hip replacement the following year and the other knee replaced the year after next. Soon after he died; his wife collected all the prosthesis from the ashes after the cremation, got a walking stick made and told to all and sundry:

"See, he still supports me!"

Doctor, doctor I can't feel my legs,

That's because we have amputated your hands.

A fat lady went to a bone specialist and said: "My knees hurt terribly."

Orthopedic: "You will have to lose weight."

Patient: "But it is so difficult."

Doctor: "How do you expect the wheels of a Maruti to carry the weight of a truck?"

Gastroenterology

An old lady was having severe constipation, so she went to her doctor to see what could be done about it.

She told him. "My bowels haven't moved in seven days and I am in agony."

"Have you done anything about it?" asked the doctor.

"Certainly," she replied. "I sit in the bathroom for half an hour each morning and each night."

"No," the doctor said, "I mean do you take anything?"

"Of course. I take a book!"

Doctor, Doctor I've got wind! Can you give me something?

Yes - here's a kite!

An ace Indian bowler with a troublesome ulcer was in his physician office for a checkup. "Remember," the doctor said, "Don't get excited, don't get mad, and forget about cricket when you're off the field. By the way, why did you let the Australians get away with so many runs? Your bowling was not up to the mark?"

A quarrel broke out amongst the various organs of the body as to who was the boss.

"Who can be the boss but me?" declared the heart. "If I stop, life stops."

"What about me?" asked the lung, "If I don't supply life-giving oxygen how are you going to exist?"

"But everything functions at my command," interposed the brain, "So that naturally makes me the boss."

Just then the anus piped in "I am the boss!"

It was much too ridiculous for words and all the organs started laughing.

"We'll see who has the last laugh." Said the anus angrily and stopped functioning that very instant. The abdomen bloated with gas and feces and the entire body was in terrible state. The other organs accepted defeat and unanimously declared that the anus was the boss.

MORAL OF THE STORY: Any asshole can be a boss.

At an international conference a British gastroenterologist told a colleague from the US.

"You Americans are so big-mouthed that we could take out your piles from the oral cavity."

"And you English," replied the American stung to the quick, "are so tight lipped that we have to take out your tonsils from your anus!"

A woman went to the gastroenterology department of a hospital complaining if intractable hiccups. She was seen by a young resident and almost immediately afterwards ran down the hall screaming. A senior doctor stopped her and asked her why she was so agitated.

"That doctor in there," She gasped, "Has just told me that I am pregnant and I will deliver triplets within six months!"

The older doctor confronted his junior and demanded:

"How dare you tell a 65 years old grandmother that she is going to deliver triplets?"

"I cured her of her hiccups didn't I?" smiled the young fellow.

A man kept his glass eye in a glass of water and drank it with the water by mistake. When he developed abdominal pain, he was rushed to the hospital in an unconscious state. Unable to elicit a history, the gastroenterologist examined the patient and exclaimed:

"I have eyed hundreds of bottoms but this is the first time a bottom is eyeing me!"

"Doctor, I have been having pain in my stomach ever since I had oysters for dinner yesterday."

"Were the oysters fresh?"

"Dunno."

"Well, how did they look when you opened the shells?"

The patient stared at the doctor. "You are supposed to open the shells?"

During a tutorial the gastroenterology professor raised a buttock and released wind. Observing the shock on the face of his residents he said:

"You young fellows overrate sex. Nothing can beat the satisfaction of a good fart."

Plastic Surgery

A woman had severe burns and needed plastic surgery. As most of her body was burnt, her husband offered to give his skin for grafting. For some reason the skin of his butt was found to suit her face best and was duly put there. When she recovered, she sidled up to her husband and said:

"How can I ever repay what you have done for me?"

"You have no need to. Every time your mother kisses your face I get paid a thousand times over!"

Santa: "Doctor Sahib plastic surgery *main kitne pase lagenge*?"

Doctor: "5 lac *rupaye*."

Santa: "*Agar plastic hum apna de toan*?"

Ram and Shyam were working in a saw mill when Ram sawed his arm off. Shyam put the arm in a plastic bag and rushed Ram to the hospital. The next day Shyam was amazed to see Ram playing tennis.

"The wonders of modern science!" exclaimed Shyam.

A few days later Ram cut his leg and Shyam took him to the hospital with the leg in a plastic bag. The next day Shyam found Ram playing football and exclaimed afresh at the miracle of modern science.

A month later Shyam leaned too forwards at work and managed to cut his head off. Once again Ram put the head in a plastic bag and took it to the hospital along with Shyam but there was no Shyam waiting to greet him the next day.

"What happened to my friend?" Ram asked the doctor anxiously.

"We might have saved him but some fool put the head in a plastic bag and he suffocated."

A man working at a lumberyard, while pushing a tree through a saw, accidentally sheared off all ten of his fingers. He rushed to the emergency room of a nearby hospital where the awaiting doctor took a look and said, "Give me the fingers and I'll see what I can do."

"I haven't got the fingers."

"What do you mean, you haven't got the fingers? This is the age of medical advances. We've got microsurgery and all sorts of incredible techniques! Why didn't you bring me the fingers?"

"Well doc, I tried, but I couldn't pick them up!"